D1102166

BONFIRE

(bŏn′fīr′), *n.* [ME. *bonefire,* orig. a fire of bones]
1. A fire for consuming bones; hence a fire for burning corpses;
2. A large fire built in the open air as an expression of public joy.

Also by Celia Gilbert

QUEEN OF DARKNESS

BONFIRE

Celia Gilbert

Alice James Books   Cambridge, Massachusetts

Copyright © 1983 by Celia Gilbert.
All rights reserved.

Book design by Ann Schroeder.
Typeset by Ruth Goodman.
Paste-up by Emily Cohen.
This book was set in Sabon at dnh typesetting, inc.

Printed in The United States of America.

The publication of this book was made possible with
support from the Massachusetts Council on the Arts
and Humanities, a state agency whose funds are
recommended by the Governor and appropriated by
the State Legislature.

Library of Congress Catalogue Card Number 82-074513
ISBN: hard cover: 0-914086-45-6
         paperback: 0-914086-44-8

Alice James Books are published by
the Alice James Poetry Cooperative, Inc.

Alice James Books
138 Mount Auburn Street
Cambridge, Massachusetts 02138

For my mother and father
with love

Acknowledgements

Grateful acknowledgement is made for use of the quotes from *History and Human Survival*, copyright © 1971, by Robert J. Lifton, and from *Nagasaki: The Forgotten Bomb*, copyright © 1969, by Frank W. Chinnock which appear in the poem, "Lot's Wife."

And to the publications in which the following poems were first printed:
The Atlantic Monthly: "Narcissi in Winter"
The Connecticut Review: "Voices," "Storm Watch"
The Georgia Review: "The Still Lifes of Giorgio Morandi"
The Hudson Review: "In Memoriam: J.B.," "The Constellation,"
    "The Empire of the Senses"
The Michigan Quarterly Review: "Return"
The New Republic: "The Gardener"
The Paris Review: "Eurydice's Song"
The Partisan Review: "The Book of Revelations"
Ploughshares: "Nature," "The Cow," "Clyde," "Moving In,"
    "The Walk," "Portrait of My Mother on Her Wedding Day"
Woman Poet: "The Stone Maiden"

To the anthologies:
*The Anthology of Magazine Verse and Yearbook of American
    Poetry 1981*, "Portrait of My Mother on Her Wedding Day"
Poems: Celebration: "Space"
Inside the Mirror: "Translating Tsvetayeva," "At This Table,"
    "By Candlelight to Babylon," "Spells"

"The Silence" received The Emily Dickinson Award from The Poetry Society of America, 1981.

With thanks to The MacDowell Colony and The Ossabaw Island Project where some of these poems were written.

With gratitude to my husband for his love.

Contents

I

Narcissi in Winter   11
The Gardener   12
The Silence   13
The Cow   14
The Constellation   15
Space   16
The Still Lifes of Giorgio Morandi   18
Translating Tsvetayeva   19
Eurydice's Song   20
Return   22
Journey   24
"The Empire of the Senses"   25
Storm Watch   27
By Candlelight to Babylon   28
The End of the Story   29

II

Portrait of My Mother on Her Wedding Day   33
The Memory of Father and Mother in the Bed   34
At This Table   35
Unfinished Business   36
The Walk   38
Moving In   39
In Memoriam: J.B.   40
Scenes from a Fan   42
From Mount Hiei   44
Black Swan at Washington Square   45
Clyde   47
Spells   49
The Stone Maiden   51
Confession   52
Nature   54

Wandering at the School Fair   56
Voices   58
The Book of Revelations   61

III

Lot's Wife   65

I

Narcissi in Winter

They open their purses
and out fall stars.

From the long earth sleep
a perfume
sweet as manure
piercing as rain.

Out of papery domes
these green ladders ascend
trusting the air.
Nothing is truer
than their plumb line
to heaven,

so rooted in a round,
brown knowledge of themselves
and January's
white dark.

The Gardener

So thick a summer man as one
of snow, he stands stock-still
in the garden

and startles me, as I pass
on the dusty street, with
his odd murmuring. I see

bare feet, drooping belly,
torn pants, for an instant
stare into dull eyes,

then quickly look away,
too late to erase the shock
of that moist mouth,

as if I'd touched
an alien life that might
reach out and know me

against my will. But his hands
placed the strings where morning glories
scale like reckless lovers,

his breath inspires the trumpets
of the yellow squash, the strawberries'
red-toothed mesh.

And isn't it towards him
the sunflower's great insect eye
turns, over the chicken-wire fence,
for counsel, for radiance?

The Silence

The child is called from the garden,
away from the pond where the daylilies grow
and a frog punctuates the long hours.

"What's in your hand?" the uncle wants to know,
his voice and the others, always intruding.
She shakes them off if she can, but now,

caught, sullen and excited, she comes
leaving, in the grass, in the trees,
her armies waiting. Across her palm,

a newt stretches its lifeline, brown palpitation
flecked with orange suns. On her moist skin
she feels his appeal for her protection.

"Do you know what it is?" the grandmother demands.
She glowers, dumb with contempt and exaltation.
Let them have the last word.

The light records her ragged braids,
one blue rubber band, one red,
and over her heart, the shadow of a breast.

The Cow

The air still freighted with her labor
holds them both, cow and calf
creased in her flank, together
the simple alphabet of bond and bondage.

Drawing close, I stared at her long profile,
her huge eye brimming like a dark tear.
In the shadows, heavy with scent of dung
I saw Hera, Queen of Olympus,

called "cow-eyed" by the Greeks; behind her
the Cow Mother of all India, whose daughters
no man dares touch. Then how, I asked, did we come
to be despised and driven? The question

flared into silence like the straw burning
without fire where the sun flamed it. Unseeing
as divinity, the cow lifted her head, turning,
her tongue unfurling, a red prophecy.

The Constellation

Stretched out and looking
down at myself
I see how I fall away into
curves and necessities.

I am neither Olympia,
athletically trim in her
armored nudity, nor,

the Odalisque, all squinty-eyed
sensuality, naked despite
her flowered upholstery.

I am not
what the painters
paint.

Moving awkwardly, then without shame,
I construct myself: points of light
extending over a dark cosmos,

presiding over
a fragrance of heat
rising from the roadside
hymned by flies.

Space

"I had nothing but to walk into nowhere."
Georgia O'Keefe

The window
supports the message
of the sky,
the droop of the pear tree.

I dream of a mountain,
waters coruscating
down its green side;
fountains, like bonfires,
leap high.

The eye searches
for the lost blueprint of the world;
I voyage nowhere;
continents thrust up.

One black line
makes snowy fields
from nothing.

Perspective brings us
mouth to mouth,
then separates us.

Smooth lemon,
close up its dimples
a network of craters;
I remember its sour juice,
you, its cool skin.

Needing light,
the dogwood discards
the vertical,
goes on its knees.

The enclosure of your arms
letting me be
all I dare
permits me to slip away.

The hand held shut,
the hand opening out.

The Still Lifes of
Giorgio Morandi

The light is my bride,
arrived at the windows
from her journey of a million years.
Now, within my walls,
shapes emerge, attendant
on her presence.

The patient groom, I spend my lifetime
on her portraits:
arranging simple pieces
differently, bottle, pitcher, oil lamp,
I repeat them. Sounds, not words;
objects which do not change but
in her embrace shift like a flame
before the eyes, animated and transfigured,
not still lifes—no more than my life
is still in our chamber,
bare of season and geography,
where I wait on her, who moves,
who in her one skin
is everything.

Translating Tsvetayeva

I speak with her hoarse sorrow,
my voice extinguished
as I bring hers back
from long silence.

I could disappear, pulled
into her orbit. Or crack,
like clay unequal
to her fire.

Afterwards, empty, I'm lost.
The simplest things look strange,
unclear. Reaching for you, I begin
to spell out my old life again.

And yet, she knows, even though you
hold me in your arms,
I'll return to her: those eyes
that tried to outstare the sun,
the mouth that *tasted the night.*

Eurydice's Song

There is no returning,
This he would not see.
How in this darkness,
Darker than he had imagined it to be,
I had sloughed off
Everything he had wanted for us,
Had seen our lives
As an endless rise and fall
Of small desires.

Not love in his arms,
But the ecstasy of a great pine
Rising above us,
Or the sun in an autumn sky—
Effects he worked so hard for—
There were those moments.
But what are they
Compared to the crystal
The dead become, growing
All knowledge into one,
And a light blazes from our sides
A light the living cannot see.

I followed him upwards
Along the narrow way, reluctantly,
As one who would be forced
To know old pains and sorrow.
How often he had sung
Of mankind's woes, not mine,
For I was there for him
And from my heart he rose day after day
Renewed to make his songs,
Adored, followed, himself
By lesser poets sung.

There was nothing I cared
To return to. He chattered
Like a child, reminding me
Of this or that thing we'd done.
Then, was it his impatient nature
Or a sudden glimpse
Into my shrouded silence made him pause?
Wasn't it a clutching unease
That we'd outgrown each other
Made him turn, as I knew he must,
The moment before the light would burst
On my sealed eyes?
And I was free, and he,
Half-divining, understood
The trials yet to come,
The raging women
And the river's flood.

Return

Just an ordinary day, years later
When she returns. This is no dream,
It's all so solid and the same,

As if she's only been called away
From the table an instant and come back
To find everything waiting.

The shops she's just that minute left,
The old streets with their familiar legends
Charm like a lullaby with every step

Until she's arrested by those remembered props:
The building, ironwork, balconies, and strangely
She can't go in, can't pass through the heavy doors

Though nothing prevents her rising
In the creaky elevator and ringing
Her own bell just to look in,

Just to see again the plain rooms,
The children running to the door,
And that bit of sky over her old desk.

She backs away across the street staring
Up at the windows for a sight of herself
And for the first time knows

Everything is over, though her body
Pants like an old dog tricked by the scent
That says it is here, here, still.

Useless. The bone's been carried off:
Her rage of grief, a death so alive in her
She'd do anything to get it back.

She feels the cold the ghost feels,
She whom history is slowly
Walking to the wall.

Journey

Where are we going, love,
in a little yellow cart called marriage,
a dog, loyal, running after,
rings on our fingers?

Broad old road
taking us to market,
the fields on either side
flatten out to the sky.

Beyond the towns
is there an ocean
we might in the end
discover?

"The Empire of the Senses"

She opens above him
Like a crimson fan.
Pulling the noose tighter
Around his neck,
"It moves," she cries,
As his cock takes life
From his approaching death.
Together he and she
Ride out the crest
Of a final wave.
The body will not last
But the mind with ease
Consumes itself:
Serpent with tail in mouth.

These lovers have shut out
All the world.
Like a sliding screen
Its mute shadow moves
Over all their deaf nights and days.
In the geisha house the women
Avert their eyes
From these rutting two
And their unfathomable thirst.
Like demons
Wailing all night outside
A rain-swept door,
Like the infant
Hooded in chaos,
Imperiled by need,
They rage, death
Their only boundary.

Call her a chalice,
Call him the honeyed stamen,
Their lust is the same:
Devour everything.
Snow drifts over
The skin of the day.
Tides drain the blue from the sky.
The winner is the one
Who goes out first,
Leaving the other
To an empty room.

Storm Watch

The locust tree twists in the wind.
In the garden below my window,
white petunias flare like falling stars.

A storm is coming from the west.
The night stifles, struggles to surmount
the heat or break it, cannot let go
or free itself.

Naked, I stand to watch. You,
sprawled out on the bed, sleep. The sheets
glimmer like snow. Your breath
rises and falls, filling the room and me.

I won't wake you. I am staring
into the dark, making the storm happen.
But if it never breaks? If all things
must hang in violent equilibrium?

The lightning flickers without voice.
To be near you will always mean
risking everything.

By Candlelight to Babylon

Features sealed in a pale mask,
how rapt you are seen from above,
like a moon fallen in a well,

rising to one who bends for water.
Lost in the wildness of your face
reflecting mine in its blind delight,

I hover, anchored to you, we two
rocking our way back to the star
whose inner heat makes our planet live,

and I come nearer, near and close my eyes.
Mouth to mouth our tongues describe
an ancient route as we return

to Babylon, unearthing at its core
all that flowered at an earlier touch,
awakened, reaching up.

The End of the Story

And she walked out into the city
leaving the house behind.
Only then did she see
how small a space she'd occupied.
Now, free, she sauntered
down the grand avenues and up
through small streets.

The crowd was beautiful at dusk,
bodies opening to the night.
On a bench, lovers were embracing.
Waiters swooped by tables.
A sullen white dog sat on a chair.
Everything was a message of welcome,
gestures she was just beginning
to understand.

II

Portrait of My Mother
on Her Wedding Day

A young woman,
lilies gathered to her breast—
the moment of the wave
before it crests—
bride,
incandescent,
even in this sepia image
dazzling me, like a wedding guest.

Fifty years later, I uncover
in the movement of her swept-back veil
the life that was to come,
seeing revealed
the cunning of those hands
that clasp the flowers;
the will to shape a world
of her devising.

And once again I feel
how evil seems to fall away
before the power of her candid gaze
while everything in us that answers to good,
crowds round her lap
hearing itself spoken for.

The Memory of Father and Mother in the Bed

A sea smell rises
from the chasm of the sheets.
I hang, suspended
in the momentum of our joining,
thrust back to them,
to my conceiving. Their sighs
exhale again upon the pillows.

Longing for each in turn,
I try to imagine that act.
He returns, prodigal
to the place from which he came.
She opens to receive him.

Bear me back now to what
was whole, three-in-one,
quietude lapped
in a seamless universe.
They mustn't become real,
those puppets. I see them,
two white shapes, drowsing
far off in an ocean's green vault,
holding me down . . .

The pungent odor
swells up again, removing
all distance, releasing me
from their frozen grip,
and nails me to my flesh and bones.

At This Table

Close as the finger
running over the blade
daring it to be itself,
we are that close, mother.

Turn to me,
turn from your sorrow.
Free me from the prison
of this table
where the stale cakes you offer
cannot appease my hunger.

My eating is like weeping.
It is hard to swallow.
Your heavy heart
refuses me all sustenance.

Does it hurt you
to look at my thick flesh?
Why do you reproach me
for wanting too much?
What is too much
when there's never enough?

You have left me
to deliver myself
with only the spoon's compassion
and my plate, swollen full,
like the moon.

Unfinished Business

Milk flows, the pact
is made. We hold you
in the crook of an arm,

skin to skin, bare speech
you'll try to recall years
from now.

Daughters, beached on our
shores, there is
unfinished

business between us,
for the sons belong to the fathers
but you

are ours by right
of need, we
whose mothers were sent

away from their homes
unsatisfied,
to live out

the stations of the house,
domestic Calvary,
languishing

for tenderness.
We turn on you and teach
the strictest

art to resuscitate
our care-starved
hearts. We

teach you to mend
holes, rents,
absence;

to tend: to bear
the harness of
unsleeping watchfulness,

pick up our least
pulse of distress;
to cook

and fetch so we,
collapsed with feverish hungers,
can be fed.

Remember, mother,
my frightened child's eyes
staring at you

lying so often, pale,
in bed, I thought
you'd die,

and wondered if
some wrong I'd done
would take you from me.

I ate and ate, to keep us both alive
as now my daughter does
straining to do my bidding.

At the breast there is
the pounding of the heart
bearing

story after story.

The Walk

"Don't go so fast," I called,
but my father always forgot.
Helpless, I reached to clutch
his coattails until his hand
abstractly surrounded mine
and towed me on.

What knowledge of me did
his hand record?
What angers were given
to my childish keeping—to await
this instant, years later,

when I'm reproached: "Go slow."
He stops to rest. Memories swell.
A small victory implodes. So brief
the time before my child
will triumph over me
for wounds I caused, unknowing,
back on our deep-rutted road.

Moving In

Hot, sticky night, the moving truck
is at the door. Only a few weeks
since your death. Your things arrive,
the contents of your life spill over mine,
disrupting my careful rooms.
The moving men stumble up the stairs.
I hear myself call, "Put the desk
in the bedroom, gentlemen, please."

Already your elaborate courtesies
and your old jokes have taken root in me.
Where else should they find a home,
those legacies? Father, I dreamed
I ran to you for help and knew, too late,
you were the enemy. What antibody
can protect against your cells,
your acts, disguised to look like mine?
I need you back to bear the burden
of your life.

The truck moves off; things settle
out of place. Passing the mirror
that hung in the old front hall,
I discover you, familiar and strange,
waiting at the bottom of my well.

In Memoriam: J. B.

I see you at your desk, see your old-fashioned
German script, the letters large and broad.
You are writing to your oldest friend, "This is to be
The night of fulfillment." The sinking light that silvers
The full-leaved trees of summer lies on your shoulders.
You sense the house about you. Now that he is gone
How alive inanimate things are: armchair, sideboard,
Painting, dish; in them a pulse still beats wanting your
Attention, your presence, to move among them as they hold
And encompass you, like the pictures
Of the family in their frames: children, grandchildren,
Those who gathered around you at his grave.
Turn, stay, for your going leaves too many questions.

"I am so ready to go," you write, sealing the letters
To the school friend, to the children and cousins.
In your garden the vines grow in decorum along
Their strings. On the garden wall the espaliered apple
Conforms its span to an apportioned grace.
The two of you loved like the birds who draw near
In the twilight, speech smoothed by time to plainsong.
"Are you comfortable? Is there something?
Come closer to the light."

Now you are shutting the doors.
Now you are climbing the stairs.
Now you are feeling how light the ties
Have always been that tether us to life.
And in your breath as you move, now quick,
Now slow, you see yourself
Closing his eyes, thinking, our lives, his and mine
Since childhood together, how quick, how slow.

You wash with care, then lay yourself out.
The pills are small stones, the water shines in the glass.
Like a medieval knight in the woods you open
Your arms to death and wait.
Who dies like this anymore, radiant and attentive,
The garment that was you, worn to translucence?
Here, an ocean away, I climb my stairs and copy out
Your words of joy, asking, could this ever be me?
Will my death sum up my unruliness, as yours
Your order and your will?

Scenes from a Fan

In Genji's time the court
went out at night to view the moon.
The moon of August fifteenth was declared
the most perfect. They walked,
they rode, they boated, to watch
the blossoms open or the melons grow.

Imagine the charm of melons growing:
their roundness, the way they pile up under leaves,
their dappled skins.
Imagine the quiet of those country lanes
where the ladies of the court were carried
without haste, visible only by a sleeve
hanging from their curtained palanquins,
as they came to pay homage
to the ripening melons,
to the refulgent August moon
casting her golden nets
over the river.

The eye is the spirit's
dwelling place, the first country.
We stumble back in time,
wordless strangers traveling here,
obliged to see before we know.
The fan snaps shut; the kimono
flares backward in one
peacock sweep. Ceremony
builds, like the bowerbird,
out of fragments.

I want a life that coheres, where
the least gesture signifies;
where chains hung from pagoda eaves
guide the rainfall to the ground;
sand and gravel lie
raked in patterns.

I go again to school,
watching the sun brush
the character for morning
over the *shoji*. A shadow army
retreats before the light.
The screen sharpens the image—the branch
silhouetted against it—a shape
that enters me, in silence.

From Mount Hiei

Rain aslant, the hills unroll
and the pines struggle through the fog
with us, up the mountain.
On an ancient site a new temple stands.
We enter with the crowds;
our empty shoes wait at the threshold.

Inside: incense, flesh,
panic, as though our bodies,
like particles, were speeding
to decay.
Buddha, a gilded Terminus, heavy and dumb,
looks over our heads, battening
on coins and prayers.

A tolling churns the air,
hauling us in its wake
to the place where a bell hangs
huge, moss-old as a turtle.
The great log that strikes it sways
in the hands of a boy, wet hair
glistening, showing off to his girl.
She tries next, giggling, fails.

Shrouded in a cocoon
of wet and fallen clouds, we wait,
then take our turn.
Our hands, our arms, connect to wood
and bronze.
Shattered, flung over the valley,
we ride the peals, tumbling through space,
to touch, voyaging and filled.

Black Swan at Washington Square

I start to cross the Square, like
Odysseus in Hades fearing never
to return. Around me,
not the gibbering dead that hover,
helpless, but my palpable kin:
the teen-age boy smashing
a bottle, fastening a shard
to a stick;
three pale people, heads shaved,
clinging to each other in a heap.

A girl wilts on the grass,
basket and sign at her feet—
    I'm Sharon, please help me, give me money

Who will help if someone
sitting on these benches judges me
the enemy and takes me
by the throat?
This is the terror
that's bottled in the dream—
the knowing steps
towards annihilation.
In the violence of noon,
disaster waits; no shadow-refuge here
for catching breath.

Somewhere in the park, drums.
A radio reports ninety degrees,
African latitudes. Entombed
in flesh, a woman obliterates
a hotdog in her painted mouth.
Heart thudding, breaking free,
I move towards an asphalt playing court
where Swan Lake's blaring
from a big transistor.

But no one's watching the ebony body
that turns and pirouettes,
arms high, wrists drooping,
in a ballerina's winged attitude.
He's on skates: thick, red warm-up socks
halfway up the calves. He spins,
flutters, kneels in Odette's
pure dying fall.

Sweat drips from the knitted cap
he wears. His eyes, fringed
with spiky lashes, like the shy
giraffe's, are raised in ecstasy.
The tempo switches, he's Odile,
seductively throbbing,
the black swan.

He's alone, virgin and whore,
man, woman, one
melting like a candle
in the sun's embrace.
I see his triumph as he darts
and swoops. I see him
in the voyage of his dream
confront his own reality
with the daring of the surgeon
who pulls apart the curtains,
baring the red, pulsing engine.

Clyde

Clyde, you were older
than the other fourth graders;
your chalky face set off
with slick, black hair,
your lips too red.
When you smiled your mouth
went thick as a slug,
and when I turned my head in class
you were always there
like a dream I couldn't wake from,
bent over your work,
those pictures you drew and made us
look at: naked women and on *those* places
dark scribbles.

Clyde, you said
you'd get me after school and
kiss me, and I hid in the girl's room
until the janitor made me leave.
There you were behind the hedge.
I ran and ran, heart pounding,
looking over my shoulder.

You didn't even care about grownups.
You sneered at Miss Pyle's freckled hands,
called her a pillow tied in the middle.

Clyde, what about the morning
the bell rang and when we went in
someone whispered you were dead.
You hanged yourself. In the closet.

In my mind, I saw you swinging
in a crack of light through the half-shut door.
They said your mother told you
you were bad, you wouldn't stop
she was going to send you away
again.
Then, Clyde, you who sat in Miss Pyle's class,
one of us,
you went to your room.
Your wet laugh stopped.
You left me to the dark.

Spells

You are so thin the light
comes through your bones,
your skin, white
as plants grown in the dark.
Ten years old, Betty Anne,
you drag towards me across the room
piled with disheveled children.
The matron locks the door behind us.

With the other volunteers, we walk out
into the summer hours—away
from the smell of urine and
the corridor's moldy green.
Then you are mine, child of matted hair
and eyes that make a ghost of me,
telling you stories, chanting
our names, believing
I can set you free, erase
the ones who beat you,
and love you into speech.

I imagine I've cured you
the time I count pennies, three,
into your hand and you,
in a voice like smoke, repeat
the numbers once. But never again.
The breathless air goes on
sticking to us like the sweaty coins
glued to your palm.

I'm silent after that
the afternoons I spend with you.
Sitting beside you, I draw
lines in the dust. Then one day,
watching you tear at a sore on your arm,
raging, I strike your hand away.
You laugh. That night
I dream you speak my name at last
and claim me for your own.

The Stone Maiden

White butterflies settle on blue grass.
The stone maiden rises. Leaning
On black canes she balances,
Stiff-legged, to the pool's edge.
"Daddy?" Her heart
Pounds the length
Of her body,
Swelling breast and nipple
Under her crocheted bikini.
He pulls her in. He moves
His hand on the arch
Of her frozen back,
Trails her like kelp
In the tumbledown sky.

Pink petals fall on the wicker chair.
She whispers her wishes.
He shivers, close to that nakedness.
Her hands clutch at the air while he
Settles her at the table
And pours tea.
Oh my daughter what has been done to you?
Desire lies down in the wick.

Confession

Paralysis has fixed you like a saint
floating in stone above the portals
that open to invite us in.
Your eyes, unchanged, stare
from under a gaunt brow. Tipped
in your wheelchair, you could shatter
if I let you fall as I stagger
under the dead weight.

The hemlock boughs that guard my door
bend over you, etching their green
cross-hatching on your sight.
Wherever you go there's no escaping
the call you make upon our generosity.
Like a widow, who has outlived
another life, you must continue on
alone, wearing forever
disaster's wedding band.

Once you drove fast cars, rode horses,
loved wild things. You looked like
Joan of Arc in search of
those to succor.
I watched you hold a young dog
in your arms, reading the message
its heart thumped out between its ribs.
You listened to my silence until
I found the words I needed.
Is this gift the reason
you can trust yourself to others
each day?

Each of us will conceive you
in her own way, as we imagine
the life within a house
seeing a light through the windows.
Forgive me for my failure
if I make you greater than you are
because I fear to take the measure
of your elations and your rage,
your bondage or your infinite flight.

Let what persists in you,
frail but intact, accept
the hesitant gestures of my charity.
Immobile, you have traveled
to the farthest edge, to stay.

Nature

This heat, like a blow,
numbs us. Together at the side of the lake,
alone, no one for miles.
Far away, the occasional boat
trawls the other shore.

The lake is vast as an ocean,
as capricious, too, calm and clear,
then raging in storms,
hurling tree trunks
against our fragile dock.

By day, mourning cloaks and swallowtails
light upon us; fish nibble our toes;
birds settle on our hands
as if we were statues,
but wherever we walk a swarming life
forces itself under our heels.

At night, after the sun is sucked down
between the "v" of the mountains,
the moon turns her blind eye to us
and the stars rise, each one
indifferent.

I remind you how many times
we talked of coming here. Then
the moon's milky rays on our worn sill
were pledges of comfort.
The place we imagined then,
we see from our tent now, a universe
where the grasses blow without interference.

Yet here, each instant, like an X-ray,
exposes bone. We no longer touch.
Work is meaningless in this
animal Eden. Our thoughts wither.
Books go unread. We don't write in our journals
fearing the empty pages that reflect
the words we dare not express.

"Nothing," the insects shrill, "nothing."
And something in our own cells
answers that call.
The waters of the lake are glacier-fed.
We stare twenty feet down
into its annihilating clarity,
superfluous, drowned.

Wandering at the School Fair

I.

Children stretch like playful lizards
along the lower branches of an ancient
copper beech. Inside the schoolhouse,
a mother and daughter are sweeping
the way reapers scythe down rows in unison.
The brooms thud, motes rise. All day
fairgoers have run in and out.
At this school, where teachers use no texts,
the children clap and stamp when they
recite the multiplication tables,
storing the rhythm in their blood.

This schoolroom, the overhanging beech
will shape the memories in a child's life,
to make a home, as you and I have formed
a habitation in one another.
Our nights and days stamped a pattern
in our cells, guiding us as the bee
guides her sisters, dancing directions
to the waiting flower.

II.

Outside, midges and mayflies dance
around my head. You loom
a dusty absence at my side and I
hover near you an ocean away. Remember,
I want to say, the fair we went to
those many years ago, just married, so
untried. We found a quilt we loved,
a Star of Bethlehem. How long we've slept
under its lambent harmonies—the smallest
scraps joined with the needle pricks of time—
but now the daily changes in our life
pick at the fabric.

You are becoming someone else, leaving me
behind. We think we know each other
and yet, can we know when opening out
is really closing off, the way, once joined,
the continents have drifted apart?
You are my Africa, I, your America.
Years from now,
will anyone recognize our common origin?
"We are one kind," I call across the gulf
that divides us, regretting what I never thought
to prize.

     III.

The air is shrill with willow tunes
where children crowd around the whistle maker.
He strips the bark from the branch
in a single sheath. Two small incisions
and it's done, a sound, sharp and piercing
as new grief. They say the Indians
blew these whistles to keep the bugs away.
I close my eyes, the sound is another time,
another way of life, trembling whole,
like a bubble on the water's surface.

Voices

For you, having your first child at 38

Ellen/Not lost/but gone before
Mary/Gone to rest/She is not dead/but sleeping

August heat swaddles the cemetery
but the slant of light warns how we tip
to autumn now. Gently, I put my hand on your belly,
five months full, hard as a crystal ball.
No child will ever quicken in me again.
I called you my Virgo sister once
born on the same day, ten years after me,
years that marked us as if
we came from different countries.

Helen/Beloved wife of Henry Stevens
She always made home happy

"I feel the baby kicking now," you say.
I'd forgotten your voice, husky and childlike.
I've forgotten many things. The distance I am
from your happiness measures the time for me—
the miles I must travel back to the woman
I was, strolling under the trees, feeling
the baby in me like a buckler
against the world's woes; dreaming
of a Republic where I would set every wrong
to right, raising the child at my knee.
Then, locked in service to that myth
as exigent as any stepmother's commands,
what could I understand of your talk
of protest, struggle—the vision
you pursued? You, free to act,
you changed our times and I am changed
because of you.

I envy you, watching you read
the Memorial to the Union.
Here the Civil War lies buried
under a sphinx with the wide, blank eyes
of a coin. Had we been born to the South, I
would have acquiesced, you
would have crossed in the awful dark
with the slaves, over the rivers
and divides, to give them life.

Your cheeks have hollowed; I see
some gray hair. In two years, you'll be forty.
Have you envied me for giving birth?
Your shapeless shape that antedates
all history confronts me.
How does a bird refuse to know
its wings? Only a few have ever
denied this certain power within
to gamble on greater knowledge.

Too late to tell you now of terrors
over a sick child, or rage at an adolescent
that shattered me with guilt, and the utter
loneliness of responsibilities never
fully shared. I want to forget myself,
the madwoman trying to get pregnant,
my life condensed to a castaway's vision
fixed on a speck.

I remember on a Georgia back road, a tortoise,
taking no notice of me, her time come,
in a pit of her making in the hot, gritty sand.
I knelt watching. The leathery brow wrinkled,
it seemed, in pain. I heard the hoarse expelling
of breath through the tiny skull holes
of her fierce beak.

Dogs, or a car could have killed her,
but nothing could have disconnected
the gravity that held her ejecting, one
by one, (I counted as they came) nine glowing
white almond-shapes—behind their walls
a faint pulsation of the rose of living flesh.

Then, kicking back-legs, she showered sand
over her eggs and filled the space
in slow motions—this ritual—as though
I'd been told to sort out seed with only stumps
for hands, or commanded to swim in mud.
Her time, set against theirs until, the pit filled,
she dragged her body over it, obliterating
her traces. And shocked me, as she stretched up
on wiry legs and lumbered off. How could she go?

Children of Peter and Lavinia Stone
John, 3 months; Infant, 11 days;
John Henry, 2 months; Anne, 8 yrs. 6 months

You stand where I once stood.
We are connected beyond the grave
to those who are taken, but the ties
between ourselves and children grown
are slack. If I had *known*. What can
we *know*? You went to prison trusting
in your beliefs. If I spoke, you would only
hear me saying *avoid pain*.
Turning to me, you smile, filled with light.
As men go to war—ignorant, foolhardy, vainglorious,
brave—so women, to motherhood.

The Book of Revelations

It is the winter light that knows us
by the laddering of bark,
by the nubs of buds set
defended and ready.

Arrived in the mountains at the frontier,
There was silence in heaven for about the space
of half an hour,
that is the silence we know
contemplating our lives:
the child who set out with a magic stone,
the friend who left saying we would be together,
the burning house that set us free.

In the winter light we are stripped away
and I am commanded to write these things.

III

*Then the Lord rained
upon Sodom and upon Gomorrah
brimstone and fire from
the Lord out of heaven;
And he overthrew those
cities, and all the plain, and
the inhabitants of the cities,
and that which grew upon the
ground.
But his wife looked back
from behind him, and she became
a pillar of salt.*

Genesis: 24–26

Lot's Wife

hibakusha: (hi bak' sha),
explosion-afflicted person. The term
coined by the Japanese to signify those who
were exposed to the radiation of atomic bombs
in Hiroshima and Nagasaki.

The moment I saw the strangers at the door,
men, without women, I was afraid.
I begged Lot not to take them in.
Muffled in dusty cloaks
they accepted hospitality
as if they were superior beings.
They were too beautiful—
faces hard and polished—
the light couldn't enter them,
it fell away, baffled.
But Lot was impressed by their authority,
he loved authority, loved
to use it. The men, we
thought they were men then,
they didn't care for us.
You could see they had a job to do
and that was all. They were looking
at us but thinking about the job.

"Sweeney was like most bomber pilots who have formed a defensive armor about their particular role in war. Their function is to drop bombs on targets not on people. Were they to think otherwise, to be ordered to drop a bomb on say, 2,567 men, women, and children, they would probably go mad. A target was a different matter . . ."

Lot and the strangers talked about good and evil
while our daughters and I served them
at table. And Lot bowed low when they said
that he was a God-fearing man who would never
do anything wicked like his neighbors.

I knew my neighbors,
women like myself, going to the well,
weaving and spinning,
raising the family.
The little boys were noisy,
dirty, and quick,
the little girls, shy, quieter,
but sturdy.

". . . girls, very young girls, not only with their clothes torn off but with their skin peeled off as well. I thought should there be a hell this was it—the Buddhist hell where we were taught people who could not attain salvation always went."

I saw the strangers look at our daughters
not as men look at women
but as we might look at dumb brutes—
no, not even that—for often we recognize
ourselves in their uncomprehending
helplessness. They simply looked
but did not see.

> "The most impressive thing was the expression in
> people's eyes . . . their eyes looking for someone to
> come and help them. The eyes—the emptiness—the
> helpless expression were something I will never
> forget . . . they looked at me with very great expectation
> staring right through me."

While we feasted the strangers,
the city hummed outside our doors,
the buzzing of the hive, moving,
agitating. Most people were like us
busy with small schemes. Lot called
our city wicked because he abhorred
the men in it who loved men and the women
who loved women, practices of love
he held unclean, claiming
Jews were different from other people.
But our city was like any other city.
And there were violent gangs of men
who raped men, and that seemed to many
especially horrible. When women were raped
that was wrong, they said,
but there was no special horror to it.

Then came the screams of drunks,
the obscene cries, the beating
at our doors.

    And they called unto Lot,
and said unto him, Where are
the men which came in to thee
this night? bring them out
unto us, that we may know
them.

    And Lot went out at the
door unto them, and shut the
door after him,

    And said, I pray you,
brethren, do not so wickedly.

    Behold now, I have two
daughters which have not known
man; let me, I pray you, bring
them out unto you, and do ye to
them as is good in your eyes:
only unto these men do nothing;
for therefore came they under
the shadow of my roof.

Dishonor and shame await those who
behave dishonorably.
We owed the guests at our table protection,
that was the custom,
but how could Lot offer
our virgin daughters to the mob?
He took the side of the angels—
for so they later revealed themselves—
or did he take the side of the men out there?

"Sweeney's regular plane, *The Great Artiste,* named by the crew in honor of the bombardier's technique with a bombsight and the opposite sex, had already been outfitted with special instruments."

"Take my daughters, but not
the strangers within my gates—,"
words spoken with high seriousness.
The house of Lot was only Lot,
we were chattels and goods.
We women were his animals to breed.
Why didn't he offer himself to the men?
The strangers smiled.
They had their orders, and their secret
knowledge: God was created in the image of man,
him only.
The rape of women and children
is sanctioned.
Our lives were spared,
because of Lot's godliness.

". . . all had skin blackened by burns . . . no hair . . . at a glance you couldn't tell whether you were looking at them from in front or in back. They had their arms bent . . . and their skin—not only on their hands but on their faces and bodies, too—hung down . . . like walking ghosts they didn't look like people of this world."

We covered our heads,
my weeping daughters and I, and ran
with Lot and the strangers through the blinding
light that tore
and shattered and broke in a rain of fire and ash.

"I climbed Hijiyama Mountain and looked down. I saw
that Hiroshima had disappeared . . . Hiroshima had
become an empty field."

My neighbor was gone. I remembered her,
worn with children, disagreeable,
her harassed look, bent back,
how she came one day when my daughter
was sick, with a special broth.
"Take it, it might help."

With every step my blood
congealed with unshed tears;
my body thickened.
For what were we saved?
To turn our backs on slaughter
and forget? To worship
the power that spared our lives?

Those who died are my children now,
my other children, destroyed in the fire,
neighbors, women and their young,
the animals, the green of our simple
gardens.
How can I spit out
the bitter root I gnaw, foraged from the rubble,
more sour than the apple, the knowledge
of what power rules our lives,
the evil that knows but does not care,
that values men at nothing, and women less,
behemoth in love with death
and willing, to that end, to extinguish
even itself to celebrate its own spending?

The stench of flesh my skin breathes in
cannot be washed away.
What life could I have surviving
the second's flash that revealed
the sight of the world as it is?
Seared and defiled, scorched
and silenced, I turn back,
refusing to live God's lies,
and will my body, transfixed by grief,
to rise in vigil
over the ashen cities.

POETRY FROM ALICE JAMES BOOKS

Thirsty Day Kathleen Aguero
Permanent Wave Miriam Goodman
Personal Effects Becker, Minton, Zuckerman
Backtalk Robin Becker
Afterwards Patricia Cumming
Letter from an Outlying Province Patricia Cumming
Riding with the Fireworks Ann Darr
ThreeSome Poems Dobbs, Gensler, Knies
33 Marjorie Fletcher
US: Women Marjorie Fletcher
No One Took a Country from Me Jacqueline Frank
Natural Affinities Erica Funkhouser
Without Roof Kinereth Gensler
Bonfire Celia Gilbert
Signal::Noise Miriam Goodman
Raw Honey Marie Harris
Making the House Fall Down Beatrice Hawley
The Old Chore John Hildebidle
Impossible Dreams Pati Hill
From Room to Room Jane Kenyon
Streets after Rain Elizabeth Knies
Dreaming in Color Ruth Lepson
Falling Off the Roof Karen Lindsey
Shrunken Planets Robert Louthan
The Common Life David McKain
Animals Alice Mattison
Openers Nina Nyhart
Temper Margo Lockwood
Wolf Moon Jean Pedrick
Pride & Splendor Jean Pedrick
The Hardness Scale Joyce Peseroff
Curses Lee Rudolph
The Country Changes Lee Rudolph
Box Poems Willa Schneberg
Old Sheets Larkin Warren
Contending with the Dark Jeffrey Schwartz
Against That Time Ron Schreiber
Moving to a New Place Ron Schreiber
Changing Faces Betsy Sholl
Appalachian Winter Betsy Sholl
From This Distance Susan Snively
Tamsen Donner: a woman's journey Ruth Whitman
Permanent Address Ruth Whitman
The Trans-Siberian Railway Cornelia Veenendaal
Green Shaded Lamps Cornelia Veenendaal